A Beginner's Guide to Trapping

Trapping Tips and Techniques

Shannon Rizzotto

Prepping and Survival Book Series

Mendon Cottage Books

JD-Biz Publishing

Disclaimer

The information in this book is provided for informational purposes only and it is not intended for use as a substitute for proper financial or legal direction by a qualified financial or legal advisor. The information is believed to be accurate as presented based on research by the author.

The author or publisher is not responsible for financial loss or damage incurred by implementing ideas mentioned in this book. The author or publisher is not responsible for errors or omissions that may exist.

Warning

The Book is for informational purposes only and before starting or running any activity or business, it is recommended that you consult with your financial or legal professional. Always follow all laws and regulations mentioned in this book regarding activities, taxes, selling, buying, or ecommerce.

Our books are available at

1. Amazon.com
2. Barnes and Noble
3. Itunes
4. Kobo
5. Smashwords
6. Google Play Books

Table of Contents

Introduction...4

Chapter One: Trapping for the Beginner 5

Land Trapping 8

Chapter Two: Wildlife Tracking Chart...10

Water Trapping...14

Tanning Hides 14

Chapter Three: Selling your Hides...20

Chapter Four: Trapping Safety, Basic Regulations, and Recommended Tips

....23

About the Author 25

Publisher..35

Introduction

Hunting and Trapping has been the bread and butter of humanity since the dawn of time. Man has taught himself how to acquire food from animals and how to properly hunt them. This book is a beginner's guide to hunting and trapping. In the pages that follow you will get a better understanding of "The Hunt" the do's and don'ts and by the time you have read this book you will have all the basic information on this fun and amazing sport.

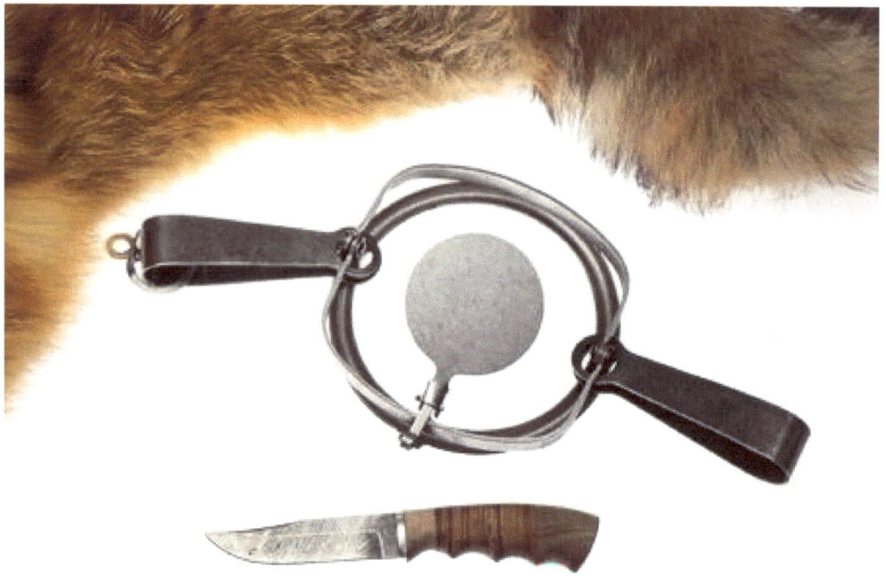

Chapter One: Trapping for the Beginner

Trapping is an art and at the same time it is quite easy. There are certain things you want to consider before you begin to trap. The first and foremost is do you have the qualifications to do so? Do you have the license from the municipality or state you are trapping in? How do you trap? What is needed? Where are the best locations to set your traps? All of these questions will be answered and by the end of this chapter you should have a pretty basic understanding of how trapping works and what you will need to have a successful hunt.

The first thing you want to make certain of before you set out to do any sort of trapping or hunting is that you have the qualifications to do so. Meaning, you have the know-how and the license from your area that enables you to trap or hunt. Without a license you are considered a poacher unless you have special permission or are included in certain Native American tribes. Every state has its own set of rules and regulations for trapping. If you check with your local state and governing agencies you will get a better understanding of what is required of you before you trap or hunt.

Once you have the qualifications that you need you can start to educate yourself in trapping. The best way to go about this is to find someone who is a current trapper or to take a trapping course. In a pinch this book will help you with the basics but, you will need hands on experience in order to gain a full and better understanding of trapping, how to, what not to do and so on.

Now, as I said in the beginning of this chapter trapping is and art and yet it is easy. The reason it is an art is because there are various techniques and general rules involved. It takes special knowledge to figure out where is a good area to trap. What to look for as far as animals go. What kind of animals you are trapping. How to track these animals. Where to place your "set" as it is called and the list goes on and on. My grandfather who was born and raised in the Adirondack Mountains of Northern New York state always said, Trapping though modern is still in its most primitive form. What he means by that was, the traps might be new but the skills required come with experience and in time. No trapper ever started out with amazing skill and sets that produced amazing kills. This is and was something that these people including myself and my grandfather had to learn in time.

Though I said trapping was also easy, that is not to say there is no work involved. The reality is, there is plenty of work involved. Here is what you need to do to start.

First, depending on your area you want to find what animals are in your area. Where I am from there is a vast array of wildlife ranging from Bear, Coyotes, Bobcats, Rabbit, Beaver, Fishercat, Mink, and the list goes on and on. Where you are from there may not be this type of wildlife so it is important to figure out exactly what you are trapping. Location is key. If you are trapping a beaver, you want to be near water or where there is evidence that beavers are in fact in the area. Scout an area before you lay a set. Make sure you have the right kinds of traps. A beaver trap is not going to be good to trap a bear. So, that said, size and type is everything. Here is a short list of traps, types, kinds, and sizes.

Mink Muskrat - #1 - #1 1/2 coils or l springs #110 to #160 body grips

Weasel - same as above and victor rat trap

Coon same as above to a #2 coils or l springs, up to a #220 body grip

Fox - 1 1/2 coils or l springs up to a #2

Otter - #2 or #4 leg hold or #220 or #330 body

Beaver - #4 or #5 leg hold #220 or #330 body

Coyote - #2 to #4 coils or l springs

Your local hunting and trapping outlet should have these on hand as they are pretty basic stock.

Once you have selected the proper trap size and type and scouted out your trapping location. This is when you would set your traps.

There are various kinds of trapping as follows:

Land Trapping

Land trapping will require you to use some tracking skill in order to set your traps. Tracking and trapping is usually done during the winter months and this makes the trapping much easier as well as the tracking of the wildlife you are hunting for.

Below is a guide on what animal's tracks look like. It is better that I show you then try to explain it to you this way the next time you are out and about you can see for yourself what these tracks look like.

The best places to find tracks are, in the snow, along a well walked trail, in mud and sometimes even sand. Though sand can be tricky because it is so loose. I would say for the beginner and the best place to set your traps are along or near well traveled animal track trails. When you are out in the wild you will see plenty of these and these are the locations you want to use for your traps. The reason being, these trails might just be the main trail to water and might be used by various wildlife that you are trapping and so as a beginner you may find this to be extremely helpful in your hunt.

Chapter Two: Wildlife Tracking Chart

This chart shows you exactly what wildlife track you are looking for. Notice on the side of the chart it has printed, Track pattern? This is how the tracks will appear in the wild. The way the animal normally walks. These tracks are not to scale. There is a description under each as to the size of the track in the wild you might see.

This chart also shows certain animals you are not trapping that may find their way into your trap. I remember as a child we had a set out and ended up catching a bald eagle. (Which is NOT something you want to do considering they are a protected species and there is a lot of paper work involved in this with your local Department of Environmental Control or DEC).

Guide To
Animal Tracks

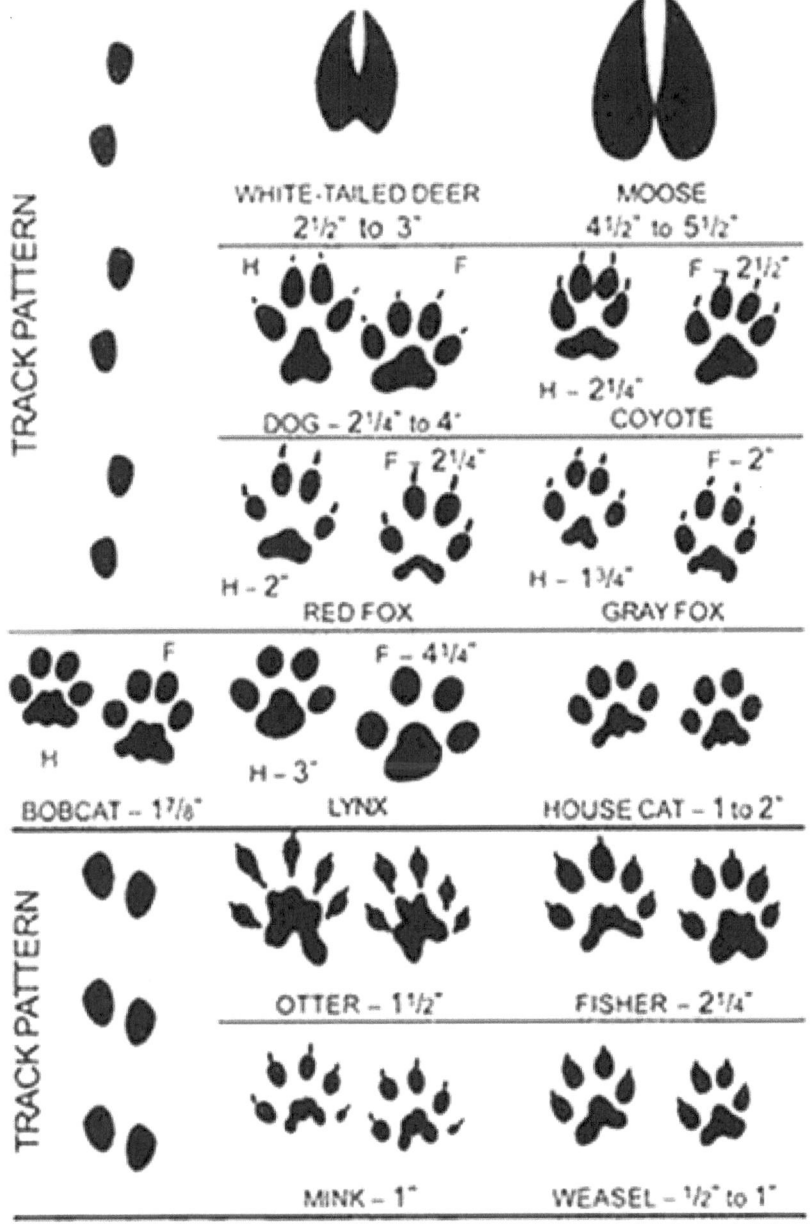

TRACK PATTERN

WHITE-TAILED DEER
2½" to 3"

MOOSE
4½" to 5½"

DOG – 2¼" to 4"

COYOTE
H – 2¼"
F – 2½"

RED FOX
H – 2"
F – 2¼"

GRAY FOX
H – 1¾"
F – 2"

BOBCAT – 1⅞"

LYNX
H – 3"
F – 4¼"

HOUSE CAT – 1 to 2"

TRACK PATTERN

OTTER – 1½"

FISHER – 2¼"

MINK – 1"

WEASEL – ½" to 1"

Tracks are not to scale

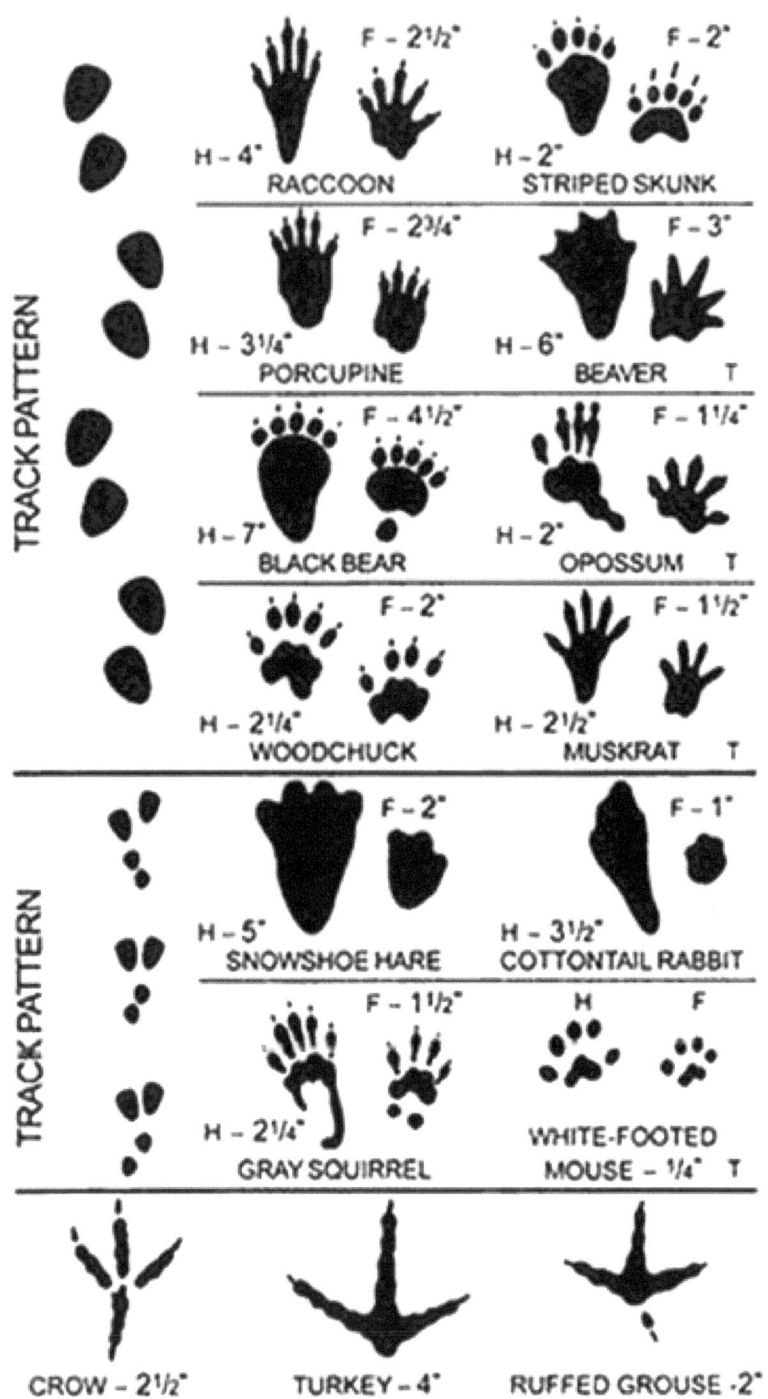

TRACK PATTERN

RACCOON — F – 2½", H – 4"	STRIPED SKUNK — F – 2", H – 2"
PORCUPINE — F – 2¾", H – 3¼"	BEAVER — F – 3", H – 6" T
BLACK BEAR — F – 4½", H – 7"	OPOSSUM — F – 1¼", H – 2" T
WOODCHUCK — F – 2", H – 2¼"	MUSKRAT — F – 1½", H – 2½" T
SNOWSHOE HARE — F – 2", H – 5"	COTTONTAIL RABBIT — F – 1", H – 3½"
GRAY SQUIRREL — F – 1½", H – 2¼"	WHITE-FOOTED MOUSE – ¼" T H F

CROW – 2½"   TURKEY – 4"   RUFFED GROUSE -2"

I used the tracks in the chart above to show you what might be scavenging in and around your trap location. The fowl listed may or may not eat your bait in your trap. The dog that is listed refers to a "Coydog" as they are known. This is a cross between a domestic dog and a Coyote in the wild.

Note: Coydogs may resemble a Coyote but they certainly are not. If you see them in the wild use due caution as they have been known to be violent and aggressive at times.

Once you have set your traps and baited them, it is important that you wait at least a day or so before you go and check them. Sometimes wildlife will come to check out your trap location many times before they go for the bait and you don't want to interrupt that scene and possibly miss a kill.

Water Trapping

Once you have mastered Land Trapping you can try Water trapping which is much the same except you are using the water as your "trail" water trapping is best suited for beaver, mink, otter, Fishercat, etc… any wildlife that uses water as its main home force. Beaver in the easiest to trap however mink and otter will work as well. The Fishercat is the odd ball out and though you may see one or two in your life, they are extremely rare in various parts of the country.

Tanning Hides

Now, once you have trapped and received your first kill you are going to want to have it processed. You can either do it yourself but for a few dollars I would recommend taking it to a butcher of wild game to process. They know what they are doing and it is better this way. Be certain you ask them to not cut up the pelt too much because the point in trapping besides the meat is to get the pelt tan it and then sell it. There is profit to be made and if you have a badly cut up pelt you cannot make profit from that. Once you have your meat butchered and your pelt in hand you are going to need to tan it. There are various techniques to tanning and the easiest is scraping and brain tanning. Some people use various chemicals to tan the hides but I find this takes away from the natural aspects of it all. You will need a few supplies to get you started.

In order to brain tan a hide you will need brain tanning solution, and a scraper. After the animal has been processed, you are going to want to use your scraper to scrape away any fat or other tissue left behind from the skinning/processing. Be very careful that you do not scrap to hard or too deep as to damage the hide. If for any reason you end up putting a hole in the hide during your scraping, make sure you sew it up promptly. Also, be certain you use special caution when softening the skin in this area. You will need a two handled fleshing knife to scrape your hide.

Once the skin has been scraped of any tissue and fat, you want to wash it with a mild soap and do it in a large tub outside. Once you have washed the skin use a blow dryer to dry the fur. Next you want to take the fur and stretch it for drying this is best done on a fur rack which you can purchase at your local trapping and hunting store. Before you stretch it for drying, you will want to "turn it" inside out if at all possible so the skin is facing outwards for drying.

Now comes the braining. You will need one brain, a blender, a heating pot or microwave, a towel, and some aspen wood. You can go to the butcher or your local store to get a brain. Pig or beef brains work best and are not expensive.

Once the skin is completely dry you can remove it from the stretcher. This project will take you a few hours to complete.

Now if the brain comes frozen you are going to want to thaw it and this is where the microwave comes in. Remember, you are thawing it, not cooking it so check it often to make sure it is only being thawed. After the brain has been thawed put it in a blender to chop it fine. Add 1 - 2 cups of tap water to the blender and mix again. This should make a soupy mixture. Once the mixture of brains is liquefied put it in the microwave for another few minutes. Just to warm it but NOT cook it. Place the skin on a table and pour the some of the brain mixture on the hide and work it in with your hands. Once the entire skin is covered you should see and feel that it is starting to soften up a bit. Once the skin starts to soften up you want a hot moist towel to wipe away the extra mixture from the skin. Place the skin on the towel and pour some more of the mixture over the skin. You will want to have the hide completely covered in this brain mixture. Roll the hide in the towel and let it set for a few hours. Chill the leftover brain mixture until you want to use it again. After a few hours check the hide if it is soft and workable then you know the brain mixture is doing its job. If it is still hard in some places you will want to re-warm the brain mixture and add some more of it to the hide and roll it up again and let it sit for a couple more hours.

Once the hide has been treated with the brain mixture and is soft and workable you want to unroll it and clean as much of the mixture off as you can. And hang it up to dry. You can do this outside on a clothes line. However, you do not want to stretch it. In order to work the skin at this point you want to work it with a steel wire brush. A soft one. Or you can use a beaver or other wildlife snare. You can take the snare and tie it off on your clothes line pole and use the wire as a pulley of sorts. The idea is you want to use the wire as a friction point to run the length of the hide over to help soften it. The heat from this process also helps to dry the hide. You are going to want to pull the hide in various directions as to work the various fibers of the hide. You can now begin to stretch it with your hands.

Try not to work the skin so much that it wears thin. You want a good thickness left on the hide after the scraping and tanning so when you smoke it (which weatherproofs it) you will have much more to use. If you do over work the skin and do put a hole in it again, you need to sew it up promptly. Now once you have completed these steps you are going to smoke the skin.

Smoking helps the hide stay soft and protects it from decomposition and from bugs eating it. You are going to want to sew the skin into a temporary bag shape and turn it inside out in order to smoke it. You do not want to get or allow the fur to get smoked as it will change the color of the fur. Be sure to close the legs as well any smoke on the right side of the fur is not a good thing.

To make the perfect smoker without having to spend a lot of money. Dig a hole about 18 inches wide and about a foot deep in the ground. Now, once you have done that, light a fire in the whole with some aspen or cedar wood but any wood will do and let it burn down to coals. Keep water on hand as you want to smoke the skin not burn it and any flame or fire will damage the hide.

The best way to properly smoke the skin is to build a tripod over the coal pit you just dug and hand the skin about 6-8 inches above the pit this will provide the smoke that is needed to cure the hide without allowing too much heat to be added to the skin. You can smoke your fur for about 30 to 45 minutes. This is enough time to cure the pelt.

Using this method is the most inexpensive way to cure several furs for about $5.00 and a lot of elbow grease. It is certainly worth the effort for what you will receive.

Once you have done this you can remove the skin and cut the area that you sewed together and pull the fur right side out. Once you have done this your fur has been successfully tanned and you are ready to either use it for yourself or take it to the market for sale.

Chapter Three: Selling your Hides

Once you have trapped, skinned, and tanned your hides you may want to sell them. Now you can always sell to your friends and family as many people like the look and feel of real fur or, you can sell at a local fur dealer. Now, the hard part is knowing what your fur is worth. Here is a list of the going rates as of this year, 2015 in New York.

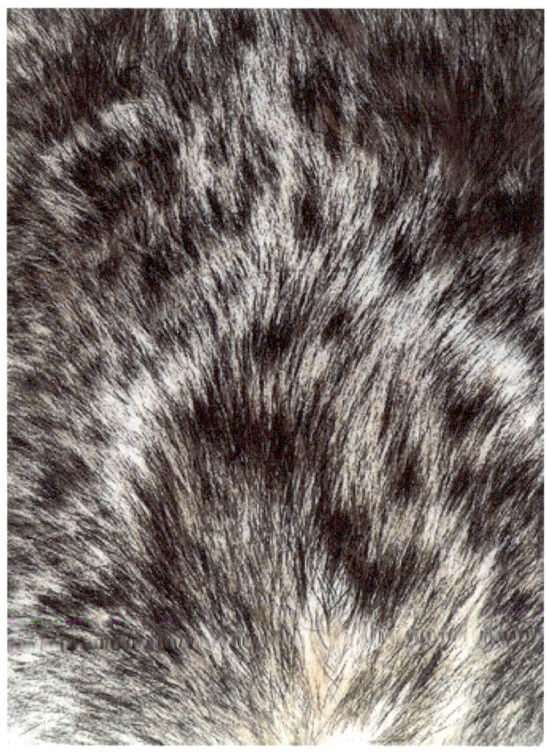

NOTE: Not all states or locations sell or buy for the same price.

Red Fox - $80.00 - Full Pelt with tail.

Arctic Fox - $125.00 - Full pelt with tail.

Raccoon - $30.00 - Pelt

Skunk - $35.00 - Pelt

Mink - $40.00 - Pelt

Beaver - $50.00 - Pelt

Otter - $120.00 - Pelt

Muskrat - $18.00 - Pelt

Ermine - $15.00 - Pelt

Badger - S70.00 - Pelt

Opossum - $20.00 - Pelt

Rabbit - $8.00 - Pelt

Selling your hides is a great way to make a profit on all the hard work you have completed. Now, once you know what the basic value of your pelts is worth you have an idea where to start with what price you want to charge for them. This said, you may find a wholesaler who is willing to buy direct from you for less which may or may not be a good endeavor if you are going to continue to trap every season. Having a regular buyer is a great idea.

Here are two buyers with great reputations that I would consider talking to if you are looking to sell pelts in quantity.

Selling your Furs in Canada

Fur Harvesters Auction Inc.
1867 Bond St.
North Bay, ON, P1B - 8K6
TN: 1-705-495-4688

Or

North American Fur Auctions
205 Industrial Park Drive
Stoughton, WI 53589
TN: 1-608-205-9200

Now, these are just two of many fur dealers and buyers out there but they come with the highest review and the fairest prices. I would recommend that you shop around before just selling to any single dealer or buyer. You may find a great deal with someone and when you do that is who you should stick with.

Chapter Four: Trapping Safety, Basic Regulations, and Recommended Tips

It is always important to remember that safety comes first. Be it while trapping or during tanning. Here are a few pointers on how to be safe while doing both.

REMEMBER: Trapping laws vary by state be sure to check your local laws regarding trapping, tagging, and selling pelts. Fines can be very stiff if you ignore these regulations.

Always obtain permission to trap on private property.

Never use a trap in any way not intended of the trap.

Do not allow children to play with, on, or near traps for any reason unless they are in close adult supervision.

After setting a trap be certain it is set correct and NEVER place hands or legs inside of the trap. Serious injury may result if due caution is not taken.

If injured from a trap seek medical help immediately. Do not try and remove the trap from a limb. The pressure of the trap though painful is what is saving your life especially if the trap has caused serious tissue damage and bleeding has resulted.

Traps are not toys and should never be treated as such.

Always make certain you are licensed to trap in the state you live. Poaching is a serious crime and may result in stiff penalties and or jail time.

Always keep your traps well maintained.

Never trap in areas traveled by pedestrians or family pets.

If you are trapping for the purpose of humane relocation of wildlife contact your local animal or game warden for locations acceptable for the release of captured wildlife. Make sure you are allowed to relocate to any area before you do so.

About the Author

Born in the Adirondack Mountains of Northern New York State Shannon Rizzotto has been writing since the age of eleven. Since then he has penned three titles of his own as well as countless columns for three newspapers in New York and Vermont. He has been the author of two series online and in print titled, *In your backyard*, as well as *Kids Korner*. He is the former editor of BBE Entertainment which conducted online written interviews with bands, models, and photographers the world over. Shannon enjoys writing on survival and medicinal topics and is a certified EMT who enjoys living life in rural upstate New York.

Check out some of the other JD-Biz Publishing books

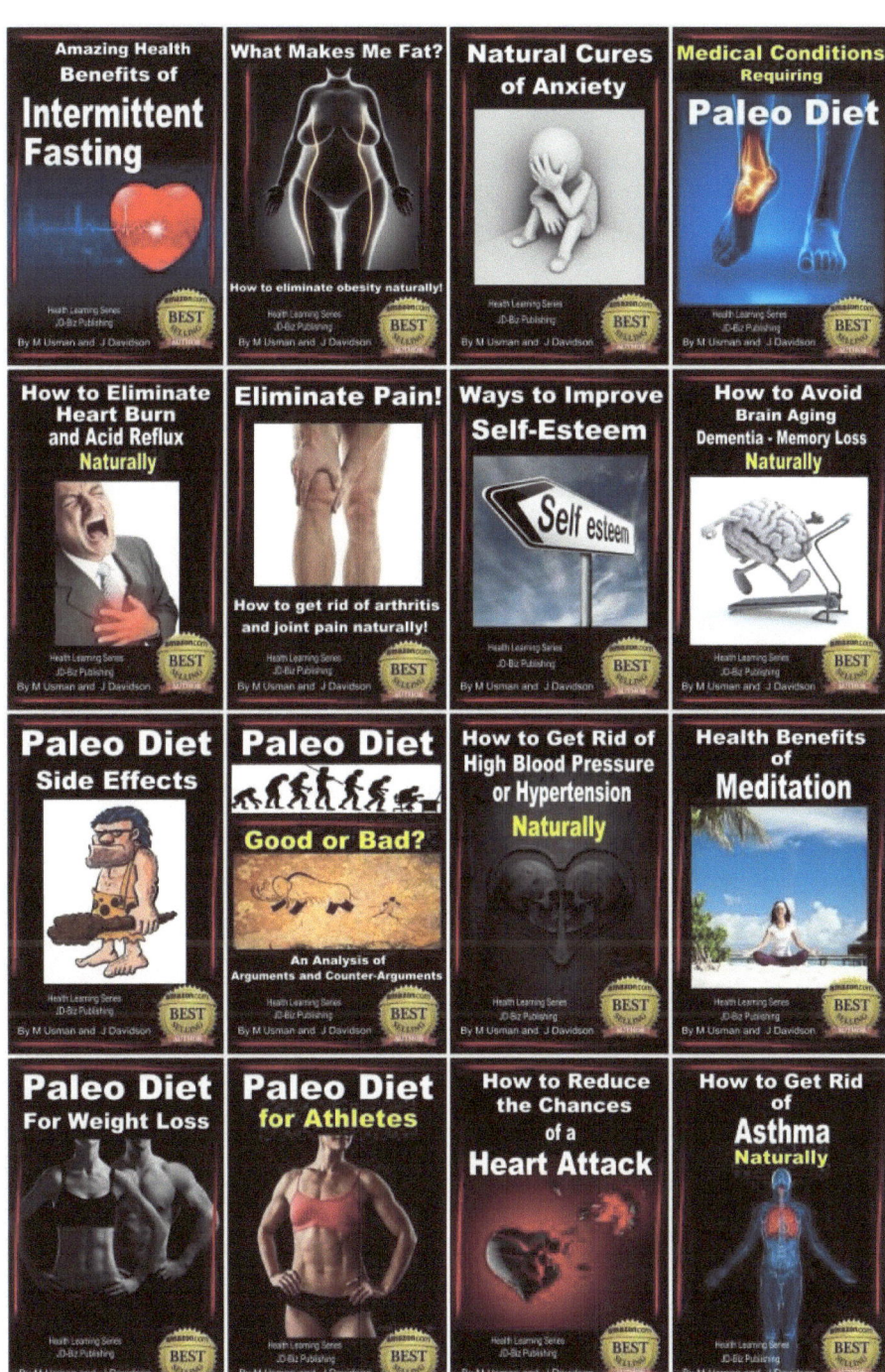

Amazing Animal Book Series

How to Build and Plan Books

Entrepreneur Book Series

Our books are available at

1. Amazon.com

2. Barnes and Noble

3. Itunes

4. Kobo

5. Smashwords

6. Google Play Books

Download Free Books!
http://MendonCottageBooks.com

Publisher

JD-Biz Corp

P O Box 374

Mendon, Utah 84325

http://www.jd-biz.com/

www.ingramcontent.com/pod-product-compliance
Lightning Source LLC
Chambersburg PA
CBHW050905290526
45792CB00002B/714